WALKING CLOS

SOUTHWOLL

and the Suffolk Coast

Number Seventy Three in the popular series of walking guides

Contents

Walked, Written and Drawn by Clive Brown
© Clive Brown 2012 – 19

Published by Clive Brown
ISBN 978-1-907669-73-6

PLEASE
Take care of the countryside
Your leisure is someone's livelihood

Close gates
Start no fires
Keep away from livestock and animals
Do not stray from marked paths
Take litter home
Do not damage walls, hedgerows or fences
Cross only at stiles or gates
Protect plants, trees and wildlife
Keep dogs on leads
Respect crops, machinery and rural property
Do not contaminate water

Although not essential we recommend good walking boots; during hot weather take something to drink on the way. All walks can easily be negotiated by an averagely fit person. The routes have been walked and surveyed by the author, changes can however occur, please follow any signed diversions. Some paths cross fields which are under cultivation. All distances and times are approximate.

The maps give an accurate portrayal of the area, but scale has however been sacrificed in some cases for the sake of clarity and to fit restrictions of page size.

Walking Close To have taken every care in the research and production of this guide but cannot be held responsible for the safety of anyone using them.

During very wet weather, parts of these walks may become impassable through flooding, check before starting out. Stiles and rights of way can get overgrown during the summer; folding secateurs are a useful addition to a walker's rucksack.

Thanks to Angela for help in production of these booklets

Views or comments?
walkingcloseto@yahoo.co.uk

73:

Walking Close to Southwold

The main feature of the coast close to Southwold is the speed at which parts of it are disappearing. This is very evident from the beach on walk no 6 near Covehithe where the cliffs eroded close to half a mile during the 19th and 20th centuries.

The Dunwich area has always been one of the worst affected by coastal erosion. A large settlement here is thought to have been the main town of the Kingdom of East Anglia during the Dark Ages. The Domesday Book of 1086 lists three churches and a population of over three thousand. By the early Middle Ages a considerable town existed here, most of which was washed into the sea. A Major storm in 1286 destroyed much of the town and a ferocious storm in 1328 moved millions of tons of gravel to block the Dunwich River, which changed course to join the River Blyth at its mouth near Walberswick. At least ten churches have fallen off the cliffs and into the sea here, the last one collapsing in 1919. An old fanciful tale relates stories of people hearing the bells of these churches ringing during bad weather; in reality anything of value was taken before the church fell.

The skyline above Southwold is dominated by the 100ft tower of St Edmund's church, completed at the close of the 15th century, by the lighthouse built in 1887 and the two water towers, the older built in 1890 and the newer, taller tower alongside built in 1937.

Southwold Pier first opened in 1900 with a length of 810ft; this was reduced by various events during the 20th century. A storm in 1934 blew away the landing stage at the end. All piers had a section blown out at the start of the Second World War, because of invasion fears and it was further damaged by a mine later on in the war. The pier has been extensively restored since 1987 and it is one of the most successful in the region. The pier houses a collection of quirky slot machines and clocks designed by the cartoonist Tim Hunkin.

The 101ft high tower and eerie ruins are all that remain of the original St Andrew's Church in Covehithe, (walk no 6). It was built when the village was much bigger and much richer. Most of the building was dismantled in the late 17th century and the present, smaller thatched church was built.

We feel that it would be difficult to get lost with the instructions and map in this booklet, but recommend carrying an Ordnance Survey map. Most of Walk no 8 appears on Explorer Map No 212, the rest of the walks are on the Explorer Southwold & Bungay area map no 231; Landranger no 156 covers at a smaller scale. Roads, geographical features and buildings, not on our map but visible from the walk can be easily identified.

1   Walberswick Common

4³/₄ Miles   2¹/₄ Hours

Use the car park nearest to the river in Walberswick, (pay and display during the summer); pub, shop and toilets in the village.

1   Leave the car park over the footbridge at the back and keep to the path ahead, bear right over the top of the dunes to the beach and turn right. Continue past the fences and along the top of the dunes for 600yds and turn right, go down the unmarked path and cross the footbridge over the Dunwich River.

2   Turn left and follow the path keeping the river to the left, all the way to the derelict windmill tower. Turn right, along the top of the embankment and keep ahead on the path through the trees. Bear right on a wider track, up a slight slope and take the narrow path left/straight on up to the narrow tarmac road.

3   Cross and go through the gate ahead, bear left over the heathland and follow the track right, through edge of the trees. After 400yds, bear right, through a gate and cross the field ahead; this field may be under cultivation but a track should be well marked within any crop.

4   Turn right, along this surprisingly busy road for 90yds and bear left at the signpost. Keep direction across Walberswick Common, go through the gate and continue parallel to the disused railway cutting to the tarmac road. Turn left/straight on to the footbridge at the River Blyth.

5   Take the path right, with the river to the left, all the way to the car park on the right ahead and your vehicle.

The port of Southwold, very busy until the beginning of the 19th century when it started to silt up, declined in favour of Lowestoft. The Great Eastern Railway consequently refused to build a branch line to the town from its main line through Halesworth. Local businessmen succeeded in their efforts to raise capital and build a narrow gauge railway through Blythburgh and past Wenhaston and Walberswick. The Southwold Railway opened in 1879 and was a limited success until the years after the First World War, when it suffered from competition with buses and cars. The railway closed in 1929 with only a weeks notice.

Features of the line still survive, most of the trackbed can be walked between Southwold and Blythburgh and old rails can be seen poking out of the ground. The railway crossed the River Blyth on a swing bridge to allow passage of tall-masted wherries along the Blyth Navigation. The bridge's foundations now carry a footbridge connecting Southwold and Walberswick. A more direct route uses the

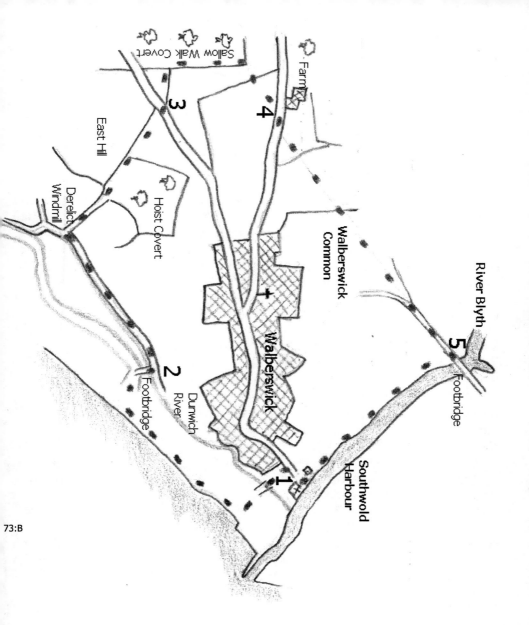

rowing boat ferry, which has been run by the same family since the 1920s. The ferry was once a larger boat operated on the chain principle and capable of carrying a car; this closed in 1941. The slipway used for loading cars is still in place on the southern side of the river.

2 Blyford Bridge

5³/₄ Miles   3 Hours

Find a parking space in Wenhaston, no toilets. Shop and post office at the village hall, pub the 'Star Inn'.

1   Start from the village hall; go up Narrow Way left of the village hall and keep straight on at the junction by the cemetery, past the disused wooded pit. Bear left down the sunken tree lined lane to an unmarked point just short of the corner.

2   Turn left there may be a track in the grass, but it may go part way across the cultivated field, to the marker post at the wide gap. Keep direction right of Low Farm, with the hedge to the right, to the signpost at the end. Turn right along the track, passing right of the cottages and go through the metal gate at the end. Take a left hand diagonal to the marker post at the hedge and go through the gap. Turn right, along the field edge with the hedge to the right and keep ahead across both footbridge/stiles and the more substantial bridge over the River Blyth.

3   Take the path left along the top of the embankment with the river to the left, through the gates and carry on to the road at Blyford Bridge.

4   Cross this surprisingly busy road carefully and step over the stile next to the bridge. Keep ahead on the path on the filed edges over a series of stiles and through gates all the way to the road at Mells.

5   Turn left, over the bridge and follow the road right at to the junction. Turn left, upslope towards Wenhaston, to the T-junction of roads. Turn left and immediate right at the footpath signpost, up the edge of the golf course with the hedge and the trees to the right. Continue into the corner and turn left, (there is a footpath signpost just ahead in the trees. Turn left along the edge of the golf course trees still left and bear right over a substantial footbridge.

6   Bear slight left, across the open field, which may be under cultivation although a path should be well marked within any crop, and cross the footbridge in the hedge gap. Carry on up the field edge with the trees and the hedge to the right, exit through the gate at the far right corner.

7   Turn left and go through the wide gaps in two boundaries to a marker post and bear right to the far right corner. Step over the stile here and walk up the right hand field edge with the trees to the right. Go through the gap and carry on with the hedge now right, all the way to the road. Cross and keep direction, hedge still left, bearing right, through the gateway at the far right and on to the road.

73:E

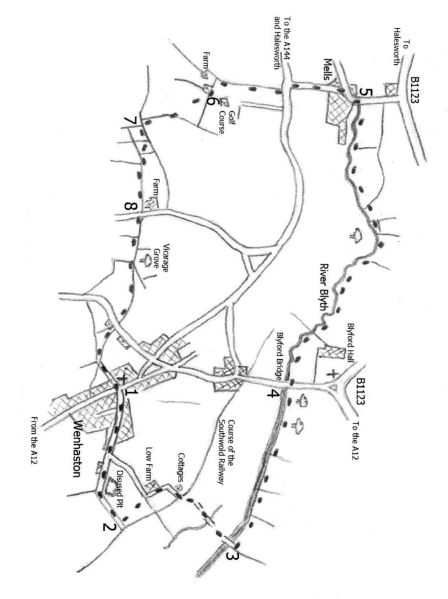

8 Turn left and immediate right at the signpost, along this wide grass path between the fence and the hedge. Bearing left, on the track between open fields and further left, between the fence and the trees. Keep straight on, passing right of the church, to the start point at the crossroads in Wenhaston village.

3 Westleton Heath

$5^1/_4$ Miles $2^1/_2$ Hours

Use the beach car park at Dunwich (donation), toilets, café and gift shop adjacent; pub the 'Ship' in the village.

1   Go back to the corner by the 'Ship' and take the roadside path to the right, to the junction by the church.

2   Keep straight on up the wide signposted path, with the cemetery to the left. Carry on past Sandy Lane Farm to the Westleton Heath information board and bear right, past a wooden gate. As this track bears right, turn left along an unmarked path through heath and trees, the track becomes indistinct just before joining another track at a reverse fork from the left.

3   Keep straight on when this track swings left, down slope to a T-junction of tracks. Turn right and immediate left up the wide sandy track between trees, to a junction of tracks and turn left up to the road.

4   Cross and carry on ahead along the road for 550yds to the signpost on the left. Turn left through the kissing gate and follow the path straight on for two thirds of a mile. Turn left to the kissing gate, go through and take the field edge ahead with the hedge to the right, continue through the kissing gate at the end, bear left and follow the driveway to the road.

5   Turn right, along the grass verge of this surprisingly busy road into Dunwich village, when the road swings left carry on up the driveway, past the houses and through the trees to the sign at the cliff's edge.

6   Turn left through the trees and follow the path left and right, through the gap in the wall. Turn right, into the corner and left between the fence and the wall. At the friary entrance take the path right/straight on through the trees leading down to the road in Dunwich. Turn right, into the corner and keep straight on to the car park to find your vehicle.

Westleton Heath is part of an area known colloquially as The Sandlings and crossed by The Sandlings Walk, a Long Distance Path running for 60 miles between Ipswich and Southwold. The lowland heath is one of England's most unusual environments, most heath is over 1000ft high and classed as moorland. More unusual birds such as Stone Curlew, Savi's Warbler, Nightjar and Stonechat are often present, depending on the season, but still very difficult to see.

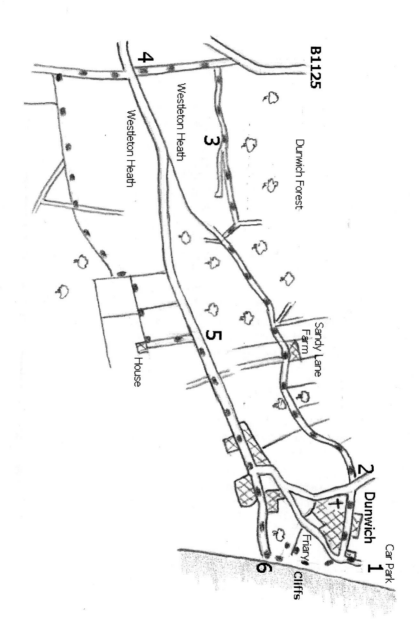

B1125

4

Westleton Heath

Westleton Heath

3

Dunwich Forest

5

House

Sandy Lane
Farm

2

Dunwich

+

Friary

Car Park

1

6

Cliffs

73:B

4 Waterloo Road

6 Miles   2$^1/_2$ Hours

Park in the lay-by off the northbound carriageway of the A12, a mile and a quarter south west of the centre of Wrentham, grid ref TM484818. Snack bar caravan early morning to early afternoon, no toilets.

1   Start from the phone mast, turn left along the field edge past the house and go through the hedge gap to the left, continue direction with the hedge now right and keep straight on between fields. Bear left around the right hand field edge and keep ahead right of the church to the further narrow road.

2   Turn right, along the road between farm buildings and carry on between the trees and the barns up the concrete, then double track farm road. Continue through Field Farm and on to the road.

3   Take the road left for half a mile to the signpost and turn right along the wide farm track past Copper Covert to the almost hidden signpost at the second boundary. Turn left along the narrow track between trees, through West End Farm and up the farm drive ahead to the T-junction of roads.

4   Keep direction along Waterloo Road for two thirds of a mile to the signpost on the left just past Waterloo Farm. Turn left on the left hand field edge, through the boundary and carry on to the road; turn right for 40yds to the signpost.

5   Take the footpath left through the trees and along the fence to the corner. Keep ahead over the field which may be under cultivation although a path should be well marked within any crop and join the field edge right/straight on. Go through the boundary and on to the wide right of way at the next boundary.

6   Turn left along this wide track between hedges for a mile and three quarters to the farm buildings at Frostenden. Keep right of the farm buildings and turn right, towards the church. Turn left at the marker post and retrace steps back to the lay-by and your vehicle.

The church at Frostenden is one of 38 round towered churches in Suffolk. Flint is the most abundant local building material, because of its small size a corner cannot be successfully built in flint. The churches were normally built with stone blocks at the corners, brought in from outside the county and cut to size. It was much cheaper to finish the church with a round tower from locally sourced flint.

73:B

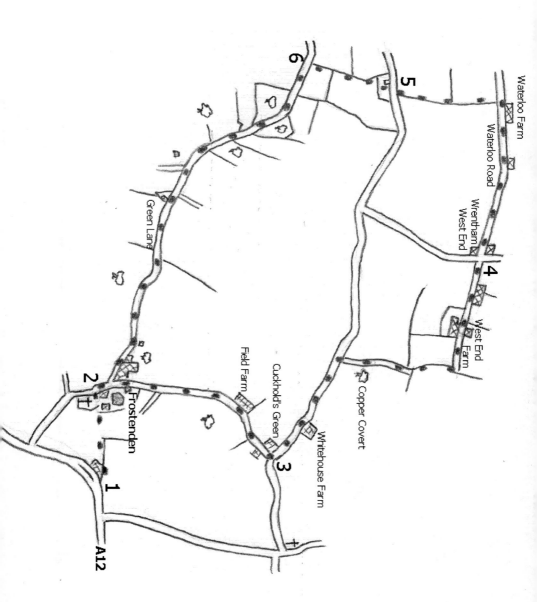

Waterloo Farm

Waterloo Road

Wrentham
West End

West End
Farm

6

5

4

Green Lane

Copper Covert

Field Farm

Cuckhold's Green

Whitehouse Farm

2

Frostenden

3

1

A12

5 Dunwich Forest

$10^1/_2$ Miles   5 Hours

Use the car park nearest to the river in Walberswick, (pay and display during the summer); pub, shop and toilets in the village.

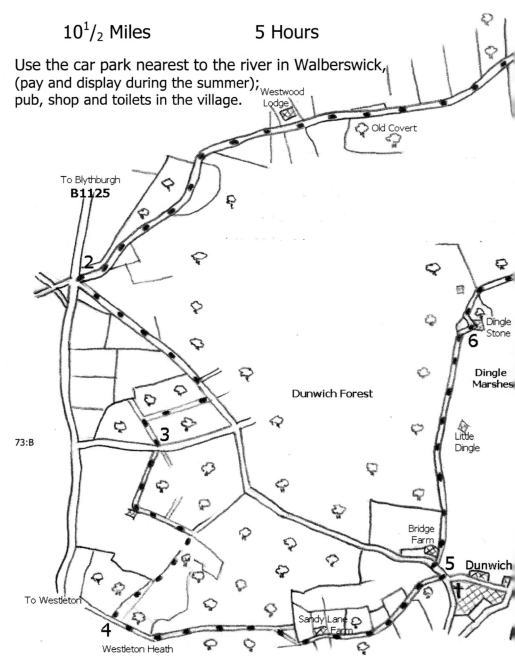

Westwood Lodge

Old Covert

To Blythburgh
B1125

2

73:B

Dunwich Forest

Dingle Stone

6

Dingle Marshes

Little Dingle

3

Bridge Farm

5 Dunwich

To Westleton

4

Westleton Heath

Sandy Lane Farm

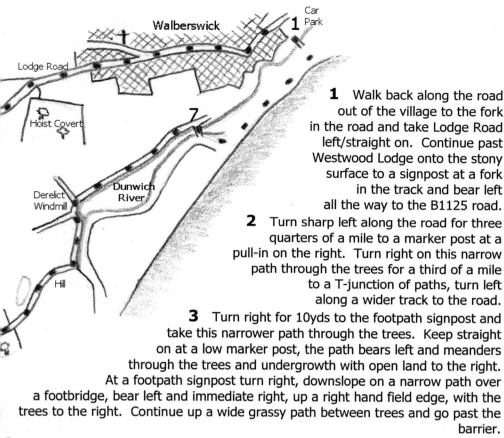

1   Walk back along the road out of the village to the fork in the road and take Lodge Road left/straight on. Continue past Westwood Lodge onto the stony surface to a signpost at a fork in the track and bear left all the way to the B1125 road.

2   Turn sharp left along the road for three quarters of a mile to a marker post at a pull-in on the right. Turn right on this narrow path through the trees for a third of a mile to a T-junction of paths, turn left along a wider track to the road.

3   Turn right for 10yds to the footpath signpost and take this narrower path through the trees. Keep straight on at a low marker post, the path bears left and meanders through the trees and undergrowth with open land to the right. At a footpath signpost turn right, downslope on a narrow path over a footbridge, bear left and immediate right, up a right hand field edge, with the trees to the right. Continue up a wide grassy path between trees and go past the barrier.

4   Take the track left and bear left through Westleton Heath, to a marker post at an information board. Bear left and follow a semi-circle back to the original bearing. After 300yds at an unmarked point, the path curves right, still between trees to a junction of paths. Turn left, along the edge of the trees, passing right of Sandy Lane Farm; keep on this track all the way to the road.

5   Turn left over the bridge to the bridleway signpost and take the driveway right. Follow this wide stony track passing right of the farm and left through a gate. Keep on this wide track on the edge of the trees, over two cattle grids to a marker post.

6   Bear right, on a wide grassy path through the gorse, carry on along this path, passing left of the low hill, alongside the Dunwich River and past the derelict windmill tower. Turn right, down steps and over a footbridge, along the boardwalk and grass path with the river still right, to a wooden footbridge.

7   Cross and follow the path to the top of the embankment, take the track left for half a mile. Turn left to the footbridge, cross and keep ahead back to the car park and your vehicle.

6   Benacre Broad

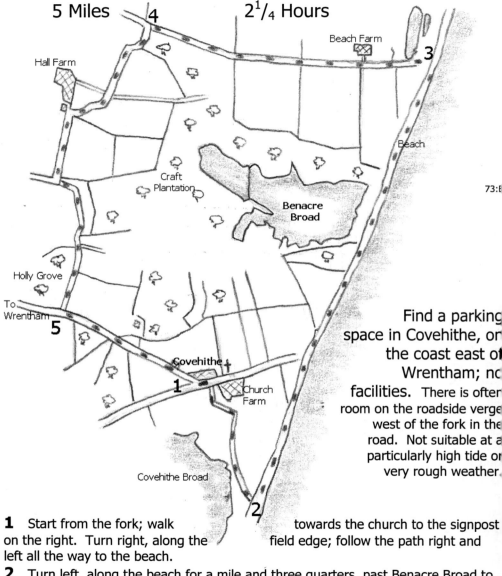

5 Miles   4   2¼ Hours

Find a parking
space in Covehithe, on
the coast east of
Wrentham; no
facilities. There is often
room on the roadside verge
west of the fork in the
road. Not suitable at a
particularly high tide or
very rough weather.

1   Start from the fork; walk on the right. Turn right, along the   towards the church to the signpost field edge; follow the path right and left all the way to the beach.

2   Turn left, along the beach for a mile and three quarters, past Benacre Broad to an unmarked point just before the small pond/lake.

3 Take the overgrown concrete track left, past a low marker post, through the kissing gate close to Beach Farm and continue along the road to the metal gates.
4 Turn left and walk around both double bends to the byway signpost as the road swings right again. Turn left along the wide, fenced farm road and follow this track all the way to the road.
5 Turn left along the road back into Covehithe to find your vehicle.

7 Angel Marshes

$3^1/_2$ Miles $1^3/_4$ Hours

Use the parking area a mile east of the B1125, south of Blythburgh, on the road to Walberswick; no facilities. Grid reference TM472748.

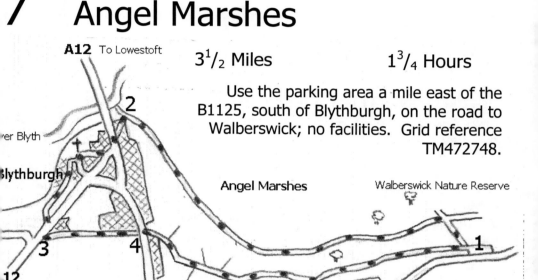

1 Go through the wide wooden gate at the left rear of the parking area and follow the track to the junction. Turn left along the path through the old railway cutting and through the trees and continue on the path with Angel Marsh to the right. *This is the disused trackbed of the Southwold Railway; look out for rails embedded in the path approaching Blythburgh.*
2 At the junction of paths bear left to the road at the 'White Hart Inn'. Cross this busy road carefully and turn left up to Priory Road. Turn right and follow the road left past the churchyard and right, into Church Lane; bearing left on the wide stony track past the cottages. Turn left and immediate right along the narrower path.
Completion on the next Page (Sixteen)

3   At the A12 cross carefully and turn right on the roadside path to the footpath signpost and take the wide path left, all the way back to the road in Blythburgh.

4   Keep ahead, slight left, bearing right on this wide hedged track. Continue along the narrower path, which leads eventually back to the parking area and your vehicle.

8   Minsmere Sluice

5 Miles   2$^1/_4$ Hours

Use the National Trust car park at the Visitor Centre at The Old Coastguard Cottages at Dunwich Heath. Toilets, shop and café, close by. Pay and display, NT members free.

1   Start from the signpost close to the Heath Barn and walk away from the sea past the end of the barn. Take the path straight on (very slight right) and keep ahead/left through a kissing gate; continue to the T-junction of paths.

2   Turn left along the path and cross over the road; keep direction upslope parallel to the telegraph poles. Join the tarmac road straight on to junction and turn left into Eastbridge village. Bear left to the footpath signpost to Minsmere Sluice.

3   Take the footpath left for 100yds and turn right, up the narrow path. Follow the path left, past the end of the trees and the field edge ahead. Keep direction on obvious paths all the way to Minsmere Sluice.

4   Turn left along the signposted path or the top of the embankment next to the beach all the way to the car park left of the Coastguard Cottages ahead.

Minsmere Nature Reserve was opened by the RSPB in 1947, taking advantage of the reedbeds established when the marshes were flooded as an anti invasion measure at the start of the Second World War. Rare birds thrive here, particularly the Bittern, Marsh Harrier and Avocet. It is also a haven for butterflies and moths, including several threatened species. Larger animals to be seen include Red Deer. Highland Cattle, Exmoor ponies and Polish Konik Horses, which may be seen are used for grazing to keep scrubland and invasive plants in check.

The ruins close to the sluice are the remains of St Mary's Abbey, which was built in 1182 but has been abandoned since 1363, when the order was moved to Leiston because of worries about flooding and coastal erosion.

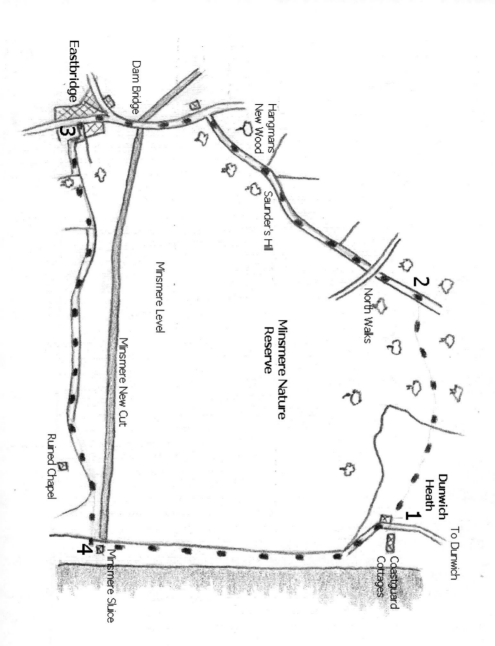

Eastbridge

Dam Bridge

Hangmans
New Wood

Saunder's Hill

Minsmere Nature
Reserve

North Walks

Minsmere Level

Minsmere New Cut

Dunwich
Heath

To Dunwich

Coastguard
Cottages

Ruined Chapel

Minsmere Slice

3

2

1

4

9 Buss Creek

4¹/₄ Miles

2 Hours

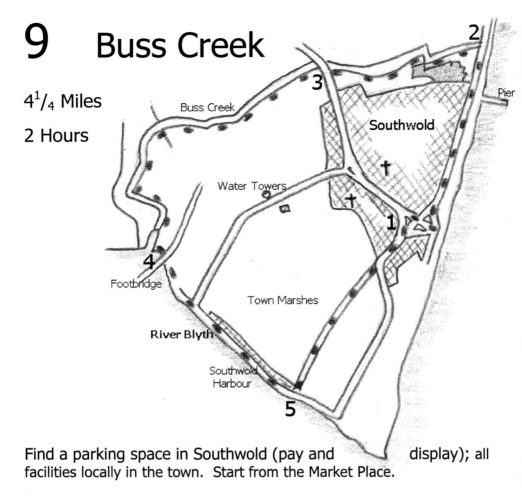

Find a parking space in Southwold (pay and display); all facilities locally in the town. Start from the Market Place.

1   Go up East Street to the sea front and turn left, down past the pier to the footpath signpost on the left at the end of the car park.

2   Take the path left along the top of the embankment between patches of reeds to the A1095 and cross this busy road carefully.

3   Continue ahead along the embankment with Buss Creek to the right, straight on over the higher embankment at the signpost, through a gate and over a stile. The path leads eventually to the River Blyth at a metal footbridge.

4   Turn left along the track with the river to the right and carry on along the edge of the harbour to the footpath signpost.

5   Take the path left with the embankment to the right and continue up the hill into Southwold, bearing left to the Market Place.

10 Greyfriars Wood

3¹/₂ Miles

1¹/₂ Hours

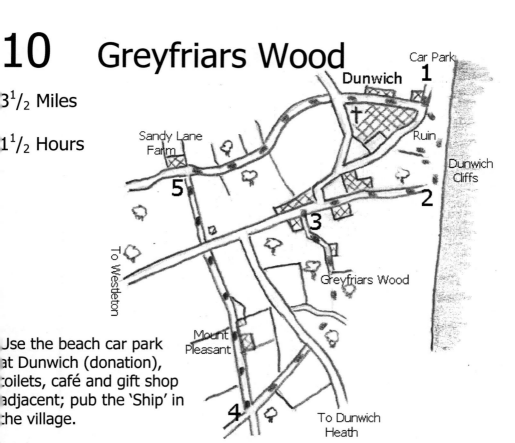

Use the beach car park at Dunwich (donation), toilets, café and gift shop adjacent; pub the 'Ship' in the village.

1   Take the road back out of the car park and turn left at the marker post, on the path into the trees. Carry on up the steps to the right, up the path through the trees and join the main path left. Follow the path along the edge of the friary grounds with the wall to the left, into the corner and turn right, to the gap in the wall. go through and take the path ahead through the trees of Greyfriars Wood to the information board.

2   Turn right, along the wide track between fences, past the houses and up the drive to the road. Walk up the wide grass verge to the signpost on the left.

3   Go up the wide drive to the left, bearing left then right to where the drive ends at a white bungalow. Continue straight on through the trees, bearing right and left past a house. Cross the wide vehicle track and bear right, to the road. Carry on almost straight on/right, up this wide path to the signpost.

4   Turn sharp right, keep direction through Mount Pleasant Farm and over the road to the T-junction of tracks at Sandy Lane Farm.

5   Take the path right, to the road in Dunwich and keep ahead past the church; turn left at the end, down to the car park and your vehicle.

11   Westwood Marshes

$5^1/_2$ Miles $2^1/_2$ Hours

Use the parking area at the junction on the B1125 south of Blythburgh where the road goes off to Dunwich. Grid reference TM450726; no facilities.

1   Walk away from the road and bear left with the main track, past the house; carry on past Westwood Lodge and follow the tarmac road for just over another mile to the bridleway signpost on the right.

2   Take the bridleway to the right, downslope, slight left and keep ahead on the wider track straight on. Bear right at the fork, continue with the fence to the right and keep direction on the stony track towards the derelict windmill.

3   Turn right at the windmill, up to the signpost and turn right, along the grassy footpath to an embankment. Turn left and immediate right, through the hedge tunnel.

4   Follow the track as it winds its way through the reeds of Westwood Marshes and eventually into the trees. Continue along the boardwalks, through the trees and the marshy area and keep ahead to the parking area and your vehicle.

Joseph P Kennedy, the elder brother of the American president died close to here in 1944. He was piloting a Liberator bomber which had been converted to a flying bomb. Kennedy had volunteered for this dangerous mission after completing a standard 25 mission tour of duty and could have returned home. The plan was for Kennedy and his co-pilot to take off and set the plane on course to occupied France then bale out. Unfortunately the aircraft exploded in mid air soon after take off. Wreckage from the plane was scattered around New Delight Wood, on the left at the start of this walk. No trace was ever found of Kennedy or his co-pilot

The church of Holy Trinity at Blythburgh is popularly known as 'The Cathedral of the Marshes'.

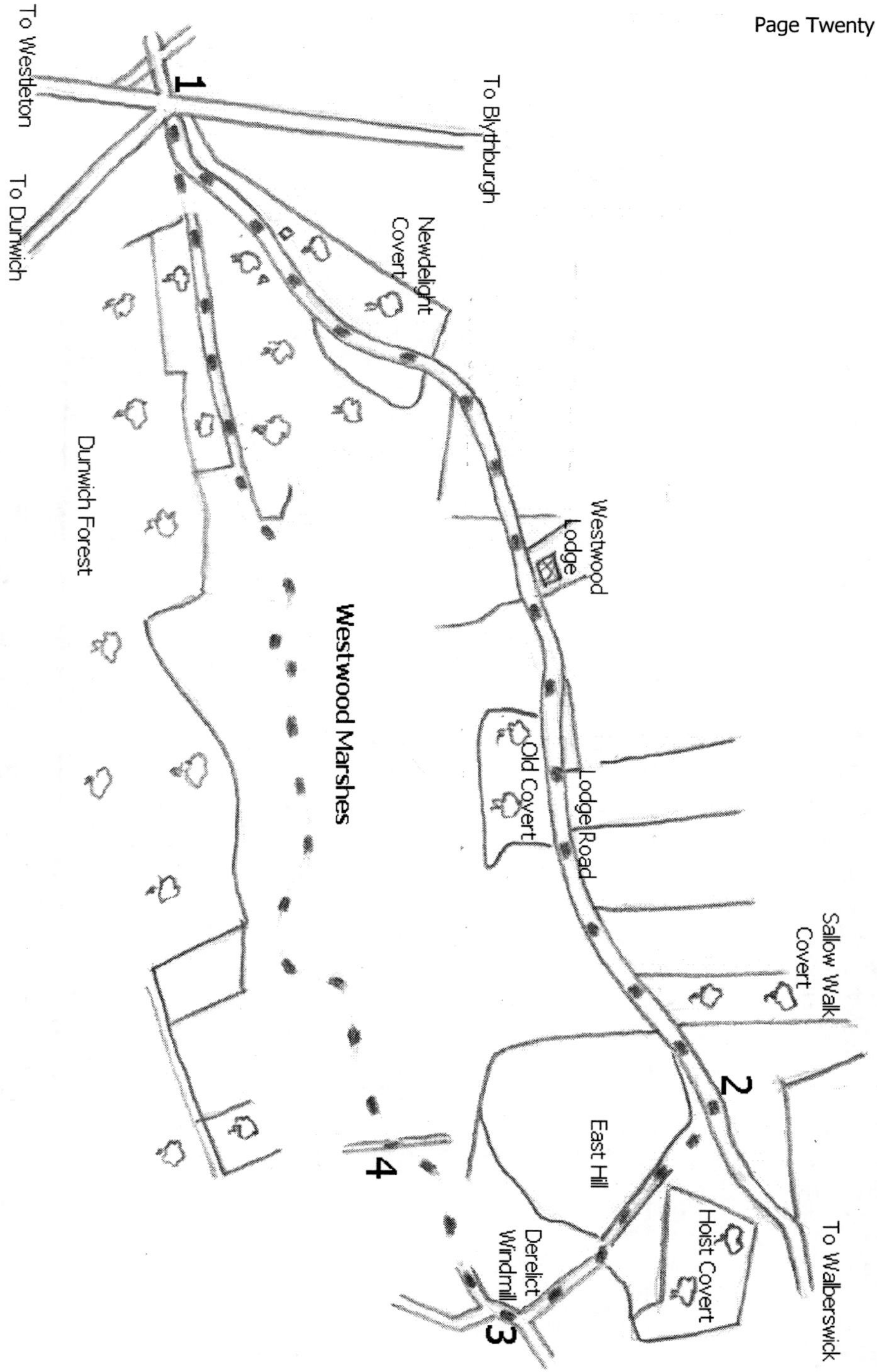

To Westleton

To Blythburgh

To Dunwich

Newdelight Covert

Dunwich Forest

Westwood Lodge

Westwood Marshes

Old Covert

Lodge Road

Sallow Walk Covert

East Hill

Derelict Windmill

Hoist Covert

To Walberswick

1

2

3

4

3:B

12 Brick Kiln Walks

5¹/₂ Miles   2³/₄ Hours

Find a parking space near the green in Westleton; no toilets. Pub the 'White Horse Inn', post office/shop and restaurant.

1   Start from the 'White Horse Inn'; go up to the top, narrow end of the green and take Blythburgh Road out of the village to the signpost on the right and bear right, through scrubland. Keep direction veering away from the road to the low signpost in the trees, bear right, upslope to the junction. Turn right and immediate left, between trees and heathland to a signpost and bear right to a narrower path to a wooden barrier.

2   Go through and keep straight on through bushes and a short length of grass field. Exit at the top right and carry on down the left hand field edge, with the hedge to the left. Go out past the signpost at the bottom left and cross over the footbridge.

3   Follow the narrow path uphill to a T-junction of paths at the top. Turn right and bear immediate left, keep ahead to the road at the car park. Turn left on a narrow path left of the low embankment to a wider track in a fire break leading to the left. Continue to the three way junction and take the stony track to the road.

4   Take this road left, all the way to the main B1125 road. Cross this busy road carefully and keep ahead on the wide track through Brick Kiln Walks to the far right Go through the gap and carry on up the tree lined path, bearing right, to the road.

5   Turn sharp left to the junction at the footpath signpost and turn left, bear right at the immediate triangle junction for 380yds to the signpost. Turn left along the wide track across the field and keep ahead over the final section which may be under cultivation although a path should be visible within any crop. Cross the footbridge over the often dry Dunwich River, keep direction (a track should be well marked) across the field to the road. Turn right for 140yds to the signpost.

6   Turn right, along the field edge with the hedge to the right and continue between fields, through the wide gap and over the next field (a path should be visible). Take the track almost ahead left, to the four way signpost and follow the hardcore bridleway ahead to the road. Keep straight on, bearing left to the 'White Horse Inn'.

73

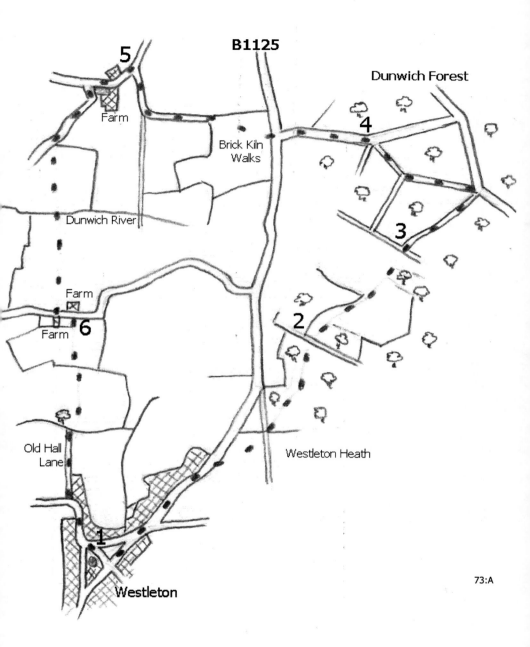

B1125

5

Dunwich Forest

4

Farm

Brick Kiln
Walks

Dunwich River

3

Farm

2

6

Farm

Old Hall
Lane

Westleton Heath

1

73:A

Westleton

The 'Walking Close to' Series

South and South West

Salisbury and Stonehenge
The New Forest (North and West)
Romsey and the Test Valley
Cheddar Gorge
Exmouth and East Devon
Corsham and Box (Wiltshire)
The Quantock Hills (West Somerset)
Blandford Forum (Dorset)
Chichester and the South Downs

Winchester and the South Downs
The New Forest (South and East)
The East Devon Coast
Glastonbury and the City of Wells
The Avon near Bath
The Avon near Chippenham (Wiltshire)
Shaftesbury (Dorset)
Bradford-on-Avon (Wiltshire)
Canterbury and the Isle of Thanet (2020)

East Anglia and Lincolnshire

The Nene near Peterborough
Lavenham (Suffolk)
The Nene Valley Railway near Wansford
The Nene near Oundle
The Great North Road near Stilton
Bury St Edmunds
Norfolk Broads (Northern Area)
Southwold and the Suffolk Coast
North West Norfolk (Hunstanton and Wells)
North Norfolk (Cromer and Sheringham)
The Lincolnshire Wolds (North)
The Stour near Sudbury (Suffolk)
Chelmsford
Epping Forest (Essex/North London)
The Colne near Colchester
Thetford Forest (Norfolk/Suffolk)
The Great Ouse in Huntingdonshire
The Torpel Way (Stamford to Peterborough)

Grafham Water (Huntingdonshire)
Dedham Vale (Suffolk/Essex)
The Cam and the Granta near Cambridge
Lincoln
The Welland near Stamford
The Isle of Ely
Norfolk Broads (Southern Area)
Aldeburgh, Snape and Thorpeness
Clare, Cavendish and Haverhill
Bourne and the Deepings
The Lincolnshire Wolds (South)
The Orwell near Ipswich
Stowmarket (Suffolk)
Hertford and the Lee Valley
Newmarket
The Great Ouse near King's Lynn
South Lincolnshire

Midlands

The Nene near Thrapston
The Nene near Wellingborough
The River Ise near Kettering
The Nene near Northampton
Rockingham Forest (Northamptonshire)
Daventry and North West Northamptonshire
Rugby
Stratford-upon-Avon
Rutland Water
Eye Brook near Uppingham
The Soar near Leicester
Lutterworth (Leicestershire)
The Vale of Belvoir (North Leicestershire)
Melton Mowbray
The Welland near Market Harborough
Banbury
South West Herefordshire

The Great Ouse near Bedford
Woburn Abbey (Bedfordshire)
Sherwood Forest
Pitsford Water (Northamptonshire)
The Thames near Oxford
The Trent near Nottingham
The Vale of White Horse
Henley-on-Thames
The River Pang (Reading/Newbury)
The Great Ouse north of Milton Keynes
The Cotswolds near Witney
The Malvern Hills
The Dukeries (Sherwood Forest)
The Severn near Worcester
Woodstock and Blenheim Palace
The Kennet near Newbury

Cumbria

Cartmel and Southern Lakeland